Greek Mythology

The Gods, Goddesses, Heroes, Monsters, and Mythical Beasts of Greek Mythology

By: Oliver Laine

Table of Contents

Introduction

I want to thank you for picking up a copy of my book, "Greek Mythology: The Gods, Goddesses, Heroes, Monsters, and Mythical Beasts of Greek Mythology".

In this book you will find an all-encompassing summary of the many books and movies that comprise Greek Mythology. Throughout this book, you will be introduced to both the major and minor Gods, monsters and heroes and some of the most popular myths surrounding them.

From gods to monsters, and everything in between, you'll walk away from this book with broader knowledge on not only these characters and the significance they once held in ancient Greece, but also how these myths and legends influenced modern culture to this day as well.

Thanks again for taking the time to read this book, I hope you enjoy it!

Chapter 1: The Greek Pantheon

Most of us are familiar with or at the very least, heard of the Gods and Goddesses of Ancient Greece. We know that they were once worshipped and that many colossal structures were erected in dedication to them. Many such structures can still be visited today; and although they are in ruins, their grandeur remains.

The mythology and mystery surrounding these Gods and Goddesses has survived the test of time. It has permeated into modern stories and influenced much of the literature we enjoy today. These beings are depicted in various artworks throughout the ages as a standing testament to their longevity.

It is important to note that the Greeks and the Romans were descendants of the Trojans. Troy was located in the area we now call Greece, where city-states were forming, warring, and creating their own expanded upon beliefs. As time went on many names we've come to know were assimilated into what we now call the Greek Pantheon.

As prominent as they are, did you know that there's actually a tremendous amount of depth to Greek Mythology beyond the twelve Olympians? In fact all the Immortals of the Ancient Greek pantheon are categorized into eight classes. In this chapter, we'll briefly go through each class, and learn more about every character associated with their respective classes as we journey onward.

The Protogenoi

Also known as the First Born, these primeval beings were the first to emerge into existence at the point of creation. They formed the very fabric of the universe. Counted among them would be the personification of the Earth, Sea, Night, Day, and Sky. These beings were purely elemental, meaning they had no bodies, but had the ability to assume an anthropomorphic form. For example, the Earth, also known as Gaia, would often manifest as a matronly woman who was half-risen from the ground. Thalassa of the sea might show her form upon every wave break, its foam forming into the shape of a woman.

Nature Daimones and Nymphai

Though the name Daimones (δαίμων) might sound familiar to some, it is in fact the early word for Demon, as we know it today. These beings are infamous for exuding a mischievous and dark nature. However, the beings that fall under this category weren't always so. These are basically lesser deities or guiding spirits, often found in nature. The forest Dryads and freshwater Naiads are some of the more prevalent beings associated with this class.

Mind and Body Affecting Daimones

As mentioned earlier, these spirits aren't always full of mischief—however, there is a class that influence humans more than their counterparts. These include the literal personification of certain attributes such as fear (Phobos), love (Eros), hate (Eris), death (Thanatos), and sleep (Hypnos).

Theoi

These are the gods who had control over the different forces of nature; they also gifted mankind with knowledge about different activities, and civilized arts. They are further categorized into nine different classes, which include:

- *Theoi Ouranioi – The Sky Gods*

- *Theoi Halioi – The Sea Gods*

- *Theoi Khthnioi – The Underworld Gods*

- *Theoi Georgikoi – The Agricultural Earth Gods*

- *Theoi Nomioi – The Pastoral Earth Gods*

- *Theoi Polikoi – The City Gods*

- *Theoi Olympioi – The Olympian Gods*

- *Theoi Titanes – The Titan Gods*

- *Apotheothenai – Mortals who have been given the same status as a deity*

The Olympians

These are the gods that had governance over the universe, as well as command over the lesser gods and spirits. Among the numerous beings in the Greek Pantheon, they are the most recognizable. Their name is derived from Mt. Olympus, their legendary seat of power. However, they are not the only divine beings that are capable of wielding such great power over the land.

The Constellations

As familiar to us as the Olympians themselves, these are the spirits embodying the constellations that circle the night sky. There's plenty to be told when it comes to each and the Ancient Greeks believed that even the twelve signs of the Zodiac were possessed by one or more spirit. For example, to them, Sagittarius was the spirit of the centaur, Kheiron.

Of Giants, Monsters, and Beasts

These semi-divine creatures are closely related to the gods, some were even made by a deity's own hand. Counted among them are the Centaurs, the Giants, the Sirens, and the three-headed guardian of the underworld, Cerberus. You'll find that these creatures play a particular role in many of the epic stories influenced by Greek Mythology.

Heroi Hemitheoi

Not quite deities, though many of them are considered as minor divinities. This includes all the great heroes of Ancient Greece such as Theseus and Perseus, Akhilleus. Heroines such as Helene and Alcmene; as well as founding kings like Pelops and Kadmos.

Note that there are many divine beings in the Greek Pantheon that fall into more than a single category; hence you'll find certain names being repeated between chapters. Take, for example, Tykhe. She is classified as an Okeanis Nymphe, as well as the personification of Fortune. Aside from these two, she is also a well-worshipped goddess among many people.

Chapter 2: The Protogenoi

Considered to be the first-born Immortals, these beings are known to have created the very fabric of our universe. Their name alone suggests this: *Protogenoi* (**protos** meaning "first", and **genos** meaning "born"). Unlike the gods and goddesses, we are most familiar with these beings were purely elemental. Think of them this way, Uranus was literally the sky above and Gaia was the earth. In some texts, they were said to have taken on more human forms or anthropomorphic (human-like) ones. That being said, these forms were inseparable from their original element. As we have described earlier, the two forms are always conjoined in some way.

Another thing to note is that unlike certain deities that govern a number of different things, the Protogenoi are mostly associated with just one thing. This is what they embodied and became the personification of.

The Ancient Greek Creation Myth

In the beginning, there existed nothing but *Chaos*. From this void, *Erebus* and *Nyx* emerged; the place where death and night dwells. Everything was silent, infinite, and dark before the birth of *Eros*. It is with his coming that order began to form. After Eros, soon emerged light, followed by *Gaia*.

Erebus consorted with Nyx and this union brought about the birth of *Aether* and *Hemera*. From Nyx sprung *Doom, Death, Dreams, Sleep, Fate, Nemesis*, and many other things that often dwell in the darkness, casting gloom in the hearts of mankind.

11

Gaia alone brings to life Uranus, who then becomes her consort. He envelops her on every side, stretching across the vast earth. Together, they produced three Cyclopes, the twelve Titans, and the three Hecantocheires.

Unlike Gaia, Uranus was a cruel father and husband. He imprisoned the Hecantocheires by pushing them deep into the hidden places of the earth—an act that angered Gaia so much that she began plotting against Uranus.

She made a flint and sickle, urging her children to attack their father, but they all proved to be too frightened, save for one, the youngest Titan, Cronos. With the help of his mother, they ambushed Uranus as he lay with Gaia, effectively castrating him. No texts refer to what happened to Uranus after, but it is said that he withdrew from the Earth or died in the process.

This act does not go unpunished, however. As he departed, Uranus promised Cronos and the Titans that he will have his revenge. From his blood rose the Giants, the Erinyes, and the Ash Tree Nymphs. Aphrodite, the goddess of love, emerged from the sea foam produced when his genitals fell into the ocean.

After defeating his father, Cronus' reign began. He imprisoned the Cyclopes and the Hecatoncheires in Tartarus. He also married his sister, Rhea, and she bore him many children. His rule would continue for any ages, but it was marred by the prophecy that he would eventually be overthrown by one of his own sons, a recurring theme in this story.

Cronos sought to avoid this by swallowing all of his children as they were born. This angered Rhea immensely, and similar to Gaia, she plotted against her husband. When it came time for her to give birth to their sixth child, Rhea went into hiding and left the child in the care of nymphs. To conceal this, she presented

Cronos with a stone wrapped in swaddling clothes. The Titan ruler swallowed it, unaware of the truth.

This child grew up to be Zeus, and for a while, he lived an idyllic life on the island of Crete. In time, he began preparing to overthrow his father while consulting with Metis on how best to achieve this. For him, she prepared a drink he could give to Cronos, which would make the Titan throw up all of the other children he had swallowed. It was Rhea who convinced Cronos to accept Zeus and allowed him to return to Mount Othrys as a cupbearer. This position gave him ample opportunity to serve Metis' potion to his father.

The plan was effective and five other children emerged from Cronos, unharmed and very grateful to their youngest brother. Cronos remained undefeated, however, and along with the other Titans (save for Oceanus, Prometheus, and Epimetheus), he fought to retain their power. This is the war known as **"Titanomachy"** or the Titans versus the Olympians. Atlas led the Titans in battle, even gaining advantage over the younger gods for a time.

Zeus was cunning, however. He went to Tartarus and freed the imprisoned Cyclopes and Hecatoncheires. Together, they worked to defeat the Titans. The Cyclopes provided Zeus with lightning bolts for weapons, a symbol that is now deeply associated with the god. The Hecatoncheires were armed with gigantic boulders and awaited the Titans for an ambush. When they began raining down their fury, the Titans immediately retreated, securing a victory for Zeus.

As punishment for their uprising, Zeus imprisoned the Titans who fought against him in Tartarus—with the exception of their leader, Atlas. His punishment was to hold the universe upon his shoulders for all of eternity. Gaia was greatly angered by this turn of events, however, and as a last attempt to defeat Zeus, she gave birth to her last child: Typhon.

Often referred to as the *"Father of All Monsters"*, Typhon was said to have been so fearsome and deadly that most of the Olympus gods fled before him. Zeus stood his ground, however, and continued to use his lightning bolts against it. Eventually, even Typhon succumbed to the young god's power and died. Texts say that the monster was buried under Mount Etna in Sicily.

The Different Primordial Gods and Goddesses

Aether – His name may clue you into what he represents. Aether or Aither is the Protogenos of the light mists, which fill the upper spaces of air. His element is contained beneath the arch of heaven's dome but is beyond the air that surrounds our mortal realm.

Ananke – The mate of Cronos (Time), she is the Protogenos of compulsion, inevitability, and necessity. Much like her mare, she had an incorporeal form and wove through the whole of creation—much like a serpent would.

Chaos – Also known as Khaos, she is the Protogenos of the lower air. Chaos filled the gaps between Aether's mists and the Earth's surface. She is also "mother" to a number of other air beings, including Nyx (night), Erebus (darkness), Hemera (day), Aether (light), as well as the birds.

Cronos – Another recognizable name due to his role in the formation of the Olympians, Cronos or Chronos is the Protogenos of time. He is said to be the first of the divine beings to be born into existence—completely self-formed. Like Ananke, he wove through creation, often entwined with her.

Erebus – The Protogenos of darkness, his element is sunk into the cracks and hollows of the earth—a place we know of as the underworld. However, it must be noted that he is a separate being from Hades, god of this particular realm.

Eros – The Protogenos of generation or procreation. He is different from the much younger Eros, a deity born of Aphrodite. The older Eros was also among the first to emerge at the point of creation and is responsible for the universe's procreation.

Gaia – The Protogenos of the Earth, often referred to as the Mother of all. She emerged at the point of creation to form the very fabric of the universe, hence her title. She is also one of the few Protogenoi who is depicted in anthropomorphic form, though it is often conjoined with her elemental nature.

Hemera – Where there is darkness, there would also be light. Hemera is the Protogenos of the day, who spread daylight, scattering the mists of night left in her mother's wake. She is Aether's protogenic consort, and together, they create the blue of the sky.

Hydros – The Protogenos of water. Together with Gaia, they formed the primeval mud. He is also often equated with the freshwater Titan, Oceanus.

Nesoi – This is a name that refers to a collective of beings, the Protogenoi of the different islands. They were formed after being broken from the Earth by Poseidon and then cast out into the sea to form tiny patches of land across the water.

Nyx – Erebus' consort, Nyx would spread his dark mists across the heavens after nightfall, shadowing the bright light produced by Aether. She, too, had an anthropomorphic form. Nyx was often depicted as a woman who was garbed in a star-speckled mantle.

Oceanus - Also known as Okeanos, he is the Protogenos of the earth-encircling river of the same name. He can be found in every river, every rain-bearing cloud, and every spring. He, too, has an anthropomorphic form. Oceanus is often depicted as a man with horns who has a serpentine tail instead of legs.

Ourea – A name that refers to a collective of beings. They are the Protogenoi of the mountains whose rocky forms were born of Gaia.

Phanes – Also known as the creator-god, he is the Protogenos of generation. He was born from a silver egg, also known as the seed of creation. Phanes is also said to have put forth the universe in order. In some texts, it is said that Zeus swallowed him whole in order to gain supremacy over all of creation.

Phusis – Not to be confused with "Mother Earth", Phusis is the Protogenos of Nature and is also among those who first emerged into being at the point of creation. As a divine being, she is often associated with both Tethys and Gaia.

Pontus – The Protogenos of the sea, Pontus is said to have sprung from Gaia at the point of creation, the same time when Phanes was setting everything in the universe in its proper order.

Tartarus – He is the personification of the stormy pit which is said to reside in the very roots of the earth. Tartarus represents the complete opposite of heaven; where heaven arched above Gaia, Tartarus does the same beneath. The name, as a place, might be familiar to some as the prison where the Titans were kept.

Tethys – As a Protogenos, Tethys is known as the "flow" of freshwater; however, she is in many aspects, an all-nourishing deity of nature. It is from her and her husband Oceanus that the earth's rivers, springs, and rain clouds all draw their water from.

Thalassa – Born of Aether and Hemera, Thalassa is the Protogenos of the sea's surface. She intertwines with Pontus and spawns the sea's many schools of fish.

Thesis – Often interlinked with Tethys, she is the Protogenos of creation and is also known as Mother Nature's caretaker. It is through her that everything continues to prosper and procreate.

Uranus – He is the personification of heaven. To be very specific, Uranus or Ouranos is the Protogenos of heaven's solid dome. His form stretches wide, across one horizon to another. Uranus was born of Gaia at the point of creation. In some texts, it is said that his son, Cronos, seized and castrated him whilst he descended to consort with the Earth.

The Creation of Mankind

After the Titanomachy, Prometheus and Epimetheus were spared of imprisonment in Tartarus as reward for fighting alongside the young gods. They were also tasked with the creation of man, and

Prometheus fashioned their shaped out of clay whilst Athena breathed life into the figure.

It was Epimetheus who had the job of giving the earth's many varied creatures their individual qualities. This includes physical attributes such as wings and fur, physical traits such as strength and swiftness, and even their overall personality.

However, when it came time for him to gift man with the same qualities, Epimetheus had run out of good things—in effect, Prometheus decided to give man the ability to stand upright like the gods did. He also gave them the gift of fire.

Prometheus loved his creations far more than the Olympians, this much became apparent as time went on. When Zeus decreed that man must offer a portion of their food in worship to the gods, Prometheus aided them in tricking Zeus. He put together two different piles; one had bones, which was wrapped in juicy fat, whilst the other had the finest meat hidden inside it. The Titan made Zeus choose one, and being unaware of the trickery; he chose the pile of bones.

This does not go unpunished, of course. In his rage, Zeus took fire away from man. But Prometheus swiftly brought it back to his beloved creations, lighting a torch using the sun and giving fire back to man. Zeus, even more, enraged by this act, went on to inflict terrible punishments on both the Titan and mankind.

Pandora's Box and Prometheus' Punishment

To punish mankind, Zeus enlisted Hephaestus' help, asking him to create a mortal of such beauty that no one would be able to resist. All of the gods bestowed many riches upon this mortal woman, whilst Hermes gave her a lying tongue and a deceptive heart. This creation was Pandora, the first woman. As a final gift, she was given a jar but was forbidden to open it. After, she was sent to Epimetheus, who was living amongst mortal men at this time.

Of course, Prometheus had warned his brother to avoid accepting gifts from Zeus, but the Titan was not able to resist Pandora's beauty. He allowed her to stay with him. In time, her curiosity grew overwhelming and the woman eventually opened the jar— thus releasing all forms of evil upon the earth. By the time she managed to close it once more, the only thing left in the jar was hope.

Zeus was enraged at Prometheus for three different things: the first would be for his trickery when it came to the sacrifices, second would be for his act of stealing fire for mankind, and the third is for refusing to tell Zeus which of the god's children would eventually dethrone him. Denying Zeus of an answer, Prometheus was then seized by force and violence, taking him up to the Caucasus Mountains where he was bound with unbreakable diamond chains. It was here that his torment began.

Day and night, a giant eagle would tear away at his liver; while he was rendered completely unable to defend himself. Zeus did give him a way out of his predicament; he could tell Zeus whom the child's mother was and he would be set free. The other two were conditions that, if met, would free the Titan. The first is that an immortal must volunteer to die on his behalf, and the second was that a mortal must slay the eagle and unbound him. In the end, the Centaur and Chiron volunteered their lives for him, whilst Heracles killed the eagle and unchained the Titan.

Chapter 3: Nature Daimones and the Nymphai

People often mistake the *Daimones* for demons or a creature of mischief, given the similar sounding name. However, the Daimones are actually personified spirits representing different human conditions, as well as various abstract concepts.

They formed quite a significant chunk of the Greek Pantheon, and their names often clue you into what they are supposed to represent. For example, you have *EROS* who represents love and *THANATOS* who represents death.

Now, to simplify our understanding of the different Daimones, they are often categorized into seven different broad groups. I'll be giving examples of each, but these are by no means the full complete list. These groups are as follows:

I. **Emotions and states of mind. Examples of which include:**

 - *Love and Hate, Affection, Anger, Sexual Desire, Joy, Laughter, Grief, Hope, Discord, Harmony, Delusion, Fear, etc.*

II. **The human condition. Examples of which include:**

 - *Birth and Death, Pleasure and Pain, Sleep and Dreams, Hunger, and Disease, Youth and Old Age, Wealth and Poverty, Ease and Toil, etc.*

III. **Different human qualities. Examples of which include:**

 - *Beauty, Wisdom, Strength, Grace, Idiocy, etc.*

IV. **Morality. Examples of which include:**

 - *Modesty, Hubris, Valor, Mercy, Modesty, Truth, Justice, Lies, Respect, Impiety, Insolence, Oath, etc.*

V. **Voice. Examples of which include:**

 - *Persuasion, Prayer, Eloquence, Counsel, Fame, Lamenting, Cursing, Quarrels, Battle Cry, Rumors, Criticisms, etc.*

VI. **Different actions. Examples of which include:**

 - *Victory, Force, Labor, Murder, Rivalry, Fighting, Contest, and so on.*

VII. **Different States of Society. Examples of which include:**

- *Law and Lawlessness, Peace and War, Justice and Injustice, Good-Governance, and so on.*

*Note that many of these divinities are purely personifications of certain concepts, and therefore do not have any mythology to them whilst some have comparatively little. There are those who have achieved a degree of characterization, such as seen in the case of Hypnos (Sleep) and Eris (Strife). Others have even managed cult status, and given minor altars as well as precincts established in dedication to them back in the ancient times. Good examples of these include Nike (Victory), Eros (Love), and Nemesis (Indignation).

A Complete List of Known Daimones (Greek Names)

I.   *Emotions*:

- Algos - Grief

- Ania - Sorrow

- Deimos - Fear, Terror

- Elpis - Hope

- Eris - Strife

- Eros - Love

- Eudaemonia - Happiness

- Euphrosyne - Joy, Mirth

- Euthymia - Good Cheer

- Gelos - Laughter

- Harmonia - Harmony

- Hedone - Pleasure

- Himerus - Desire

- Lyssa - Rage

- Neicus - Quarrel

- Nemesis - Indignation

- Oizys - Misery

- Penthus - Mourning

- Philia - Friendship

- Phobos - Fear, Panic

- Phrice - Horror

- Pothus - Longing

- Phthonus - Jealousy

- Styx - Hate

- Zelus - Envy

II. *The Human Condition:*

- Achos - Pain

- Amechania - Helplessness

- Anance - Necessity

- Aporia - Want

- Caerus - Opportunity

- Euthenia - Prosperity

- Eutychia - Good Luck

- Hebe - Youth

- Geras - Old Age

- Hygeia - Good Health

- Hypnos - Sleep

- Ker - Death

- Lethe - Forgetfulness

- Limos - Hunger

- Mania - Madness

- Methe - Drunkenness

- Mnemosyne - Memory

- Moira - Fate

- Morus - Doom
- Nosos - Disease
- Oneirus - Dream
- Penia - Poverty
- Plutus - Wealth

- Ponos - Toil
- Ptocheia - Beggary
- Soteria - Safety
- Thanatos - Death
- Tyche - Fortune

III. *Personal Qualities*:

- Aglaea - Glory
- Alce - Strength
- Calleis - Beauty
- Charis - Grace
- Coalemus - Stupidity

- Cratus - Strength
- Dolus - Guile
- Sophia - Wisdom
- Techne - Skill
- Zelus – Competitiveness

IV. *Morality*:

- Adephagia - Gluttony
- Aedos - Respect
- Aergia - Laziness

- Aeschyne - Modesty
- Aletheia - Truth
- Anaideia - Ruthlessness

Greek Mythology

- Apate - Deceit
- Arete - Virtue
- Ate - Delusion
- Corus - Insolence
- Dike - Justice
- Dyssebia - Impiety
- Eleus - Mercy
- Epiphron - Prudence
- Eucleia - Good Repute
- Eupraxia - Conduct
- Eusebia - Piety

- Horcus - Oath
- Hybris - Arrogance
- Peitharchia - Obedience
- Philophrosyne - Kindliness
- Phonus - Murder
- Pistis - Trust
- Pseudologus - Lies
- Sophrosyne - Self-Control
- Thrasus - Rashness

V.   *Voice and Sound*:

- Alala - Battle-Cry
- Aletheia - Truth
- Amphilogia - Dispute

- Angelia - Message
- Ara - Curse
- Calliope - Eloquence

- Eupheme - Praise

- Gelus - Laughter

- Hedylogus - Sweet-Talk

- Hesychia - Quiet

- Homadus - Battle-Din

- Horcus - Oath

- Litae - Prayer

- Metis - Counsel

- Momus - Mockery

- Musica - Music

- Neicus - Quarrel

- Paregoros - Consolation

- Peitho - Persuasion

- Pheme - Rumour

- Prophasis - Excuse

VI.   *Actions and Events:*

- Agon - Contest

- Alastor - Blood Feud

- Androctasia - Slaughter

- Bia - Force

- Hormes - Effort

- Hysmina - Fighting

- Ioke - Onslaught

- Mache - Battle

- Nike - Victory

- Palioxis - Retreat

- Phonos - Murder

- Poine - Retribution

- Pompe - Procession

- Praxidice - Exact Justice

- Proioxis - Pursuit

- Telete - Initiation

- Thalia - Festivity

VII. *State of Society:*

- Democracia - Democracy

- Dike - Justice

- Dysnomia - Lawlessness

- Ececheria - Armistice

- Eirene - Peace

- Eunomia - Good Order

- Harmonia - Harmony

- Homonoea - Concord

- Nomos - Law

- Polemus - War

- Themis - Custom

The Nymphai (Nymphs)

The Nymphai, also known as the nymphs, were considered to be minor nature goddesses who are found all over the earth. Despite the fact that they were ranked lower when compared to the Theoi or the gods, they were still called upon to attend the different assemblies that took place on Olympus.

The Nymphai presided over many different natural places and phenomena, including meadows, clouds, springs, forests, beaches, and so on. They were also given the care of different flora and fauna, often closely associated with the Olympian gods who presided over nature. In fact, texts mention that Artemis often hunted with a group of nymphs who escorted her during the trips.

These Nymphs are all female, but they had male counterparts in the form of *the Satyrs, Potamoi, Tritons, and Panes.*

The Different Classes of Nymphs

Anthusae – The Nymphs of the flowers. They are often considered to be similar to the Leimenides, a category of Oceanid.

Aurae – The Nymphs of the cooling breezes. They were the daughters of Boreas, the wind-god.

Bacchae – The companions of Dionysus. They were also often referred to as Bacchic Nymphs or Thyiades.

Crenaeae – The Nymphs of fountains and wells.

Dryads – The most recognizable of all the Nymphs, they presided over the forests and its trees. Some of them had their own life force closely tied to a specific tree, often the loftiest ones in a forest, or ones that are located in a sacred grove for the gods. The Dryads of Mountain Pines are referred to as Oreads, those of Ash-trees are called Meliae, the oak nymphs were called Hamadryads, and the fruit trees had their Meliades.

Epimelides – Also often referred to as Epimeliades, these are the nymphs of highland pasture and protectors of sheep-flocks. They are also associated with the Oceanids.

Haliae – These are the nymphs of the sea, the rocky shores, and the sands. They were protectors of the different schools of fish, as well as other sea creatures. Among them, the most popular in text would be the fifty Nereids.

Heleionomae – These are the Naiad nymphs of the different wetlands and fresh-water marshes.

Lampades – These are the torch-bearing nymphs who resided in the underworld. They are governed by the goddesses of the Eleusinian Mysteries, Hecate and Persephone.

Leimenides – These are the nymphs of the water meadows, the pastures which are lush with flowers and grass. They are also associated with Oceanids.

Limnatides – The Naiad nymphs of the different lakes.

Maenads – The frenzied nymphs often associated with Dionysus' entourage. They are also often referred to as Thyiads. This collective is often comprised of a mix of Naiad and Dryad nymphs.

Meliae – The nymphs of bees, honey, and honeydew. They are also the Dryads of Mountain Ash. In some texts, they are often referred to a Melissae.

Naiads – Also known as Naiades, these are the nymphs of any fresh-water body, including fountains, springs, streams, lakes, and rivers. They are often referred to as the daughters of Okeanos, as well as the different River-Gods.

Nereids – The collective name for the fifty Haliad sea-nymphs.

Oceanids – These are the nymphs who presided over the different sources of fresh water, including those found on earth and in the heavens. This means they protected the streams, and fountains, as well as the rain-clouds. They were daughters of Okeanos (Oceanus) and sisters of the River-Gods.

The Nereids (Nymphs of the Sea)

They were the daughters of Nereus or the old man of the sea.

They were goddesses who governed over the sea's bounty and also protected the fishermen, as well as the sailors, often coming to their aid in times of distress.

As individuals, the fifty Nereids also represented the different facets of the sea: from sea foam to the salty brine, to the waves, the currents, the sand, rocks, and even the skills, which the seamen possessed.

It is said that they lived with their elderly father in a grotto, which can be found at the very bottom of the Aegean Sea. In many texts, Thetis is referred to as their unofficial leader, whilst Amphitrite was Poseidon's Queen consort.

Like many nymphs in Greek Mythology, they are often referred to as beautiful, youthful maidens. In ancient art, they are shown riding small dolphins or hippokampoi, whilst holding small fish in their hands.

Their name, Nereids, means "Wet Ones" taken from the Greek word "nêros" which means wet. However, some texts also translate the meaning of their collective name to: "Daughters of Nereus".

The Fifty Nereids

Agaue	Erato	Hipponoe
Aktaia	Euagore	Hippothoe
Amatheia	Euarne	Iaira
Amphinome	Euadora	Ianassa
Amphitoe	Eukrante	Ianeira
Amphitrite	Eulimene	Ione
Apseudes	Eumolpe	Kallianassa
Autonoe	Eunkie	Kallianera
Dero	Eupompe	Kalypso
Dexamene	Galatea	Keto
Dione	Galene	Klaia
Doris	Glauke	Klymene
Doto	Glaukonome	Kranto
Dynamene	Halia	Kymatolege
Eione	Halimede	Kymodoke

Kymothoe	Nesaie	Poulynoe
Laomedeia	Neso	Pronoe
Leagore	Oreithyia	Proto
Limnoreia	Panopeia	Protomedeia
Lysianassa	Pasithea	Psamathe
Maira	Pherousa	Sao
Melite	Plexaure	Speio
Menippe	Ploto	Thaleia
Nausithoe	Polynome	Themisto
Nemertes	Pontomedusa	Thetis
Neomeris	Pontoporeia	Thoe

The Nereids and the Sacrifice of Andromeda

The Nereids are oft mentioned in many different stories, but the most popular one would be about the sacrifice of Andromeda. As with many tales in Greek mythology, this too began because of mankind's hubris. A king's wife, Cassiopeia, had challenged the Nereids in beauty; going as far as saying that she alone outdid them all.

Of course, this enraged the Nereids, and Poseidon, sympathetic of their anger sent a flood upon the land, which Cassiopeia presided over with her husband. Along with this tide emerged a sea monster, threatening to cause far greater damage.

The Oracle of Ammon prophesied that the Nereids and Poseidon would be appeased if Cassiopeia were to sacrifice his daughter,

Andromeda. Texts say that she was to be offered to the monster as a meal. She was a daughter paying for own mother's hubris.

Fortunately, the hero Perseus came to her aid wearing Hermes' winged sandals. Cassiopeia's act does not go completely unpunished, however. For it, she was placed among the constellations.

Source: *Pseudo-Apollodorus, Bibliotheca 2. 43 (trans. Aldrich) (Greek mythographer C2nd A.D)*

*Note that some texts have alternate versions of this story. In others, Cassiopeia boasted that it was her daughter, Andromeda, who had beauty that surpassed that of the Nereids. One theme remains the same, however, and that is Andromeda being sacrificed to the sea-monster with Perseus coming to rescue her.

The Satyrs (Satyroi)

As previously mentioned, the Nymphai are a class of female

nature goddesses, and that they have male counterparts in the form of the Satyrs and the Tritons.

The Satyrs, also known as the Satyroi, were known to be rustic fertility spirits who resided in the wilds and in the countryside.

They are known to often consort with the Nymphai, and similar to them, were also companions of the various gods such as Hermes, Dionysus, Gaia, Pan, Hephaestus, and Rhea.

In art, the Satyrs were often shown as animal-like men who had pug noses, asinine ears, and reclining hairlines. They also had the tails of horses, and are often depicted to have erect members. As companions of the wine-god Dionysus, they were typically shown to be dancing, playing the flute, drinking, or sporting with the Maenads.

There are different classifications for the Satyroi as well:

- *Panes* - These were the goat-legged Satyrs often depicted in art.

- *Seilenoi* - The elderly satyrs.

- *Satyriskoi* – The child satyrs.

- *Tityroi* – The flute-playing satyrs.

In Ancient Greece, actors who played the role of Satyroi in different festivals honoring the god Dionysus would often dress up as Panes hence making this the most popular image associated with the beings.

As divine beings, Satyrs are known to preside or represent fertility. Their symbols included: double flute, the drinking horn, and the wineskin.

The Tritons (Tritones)

As counterpart to the Nymphai of the sea, the Tritons, also known as Tritones, were a collective of fishtailed Daimones or sea-gods. They are often found in Poseidon's entourage and are known to be the Satyroi of the Sea. The Tritons were also the plurification of the god, Triton, whose image is the most recognizable for this particular type of nature god. Another breed of Tritones known as the Ikhthyokentauroi, also known as the sea-centaurs, had the upper bodies of men and the lower bodies of *Hippokampoi.

In several texts, they make mention that a monstrous Triton-like creature was witnessed by seafarers of that time. One of the most famous cases of which was a dead specimen that washed up and was subsequently preserved by the town of Tanagra.

Hippokampoi: Fishtailed horses/seahorses.

The god, **Triton**, was born of Poseidon and Amphitrite. The god dwelt with his parents in a golden palace deep in the bottom of the sea. As a collective, their appearance is said to be like so:

- Green haired

- Had very fine yet hard scales on their bodies and tails

- Sea-green eyes

- Tails as powerful as a dolphin's

They are also mentioned in poetry, where they are said to blow their trumpets at Poseidon's command, effectively soothing the sea's ever-restless waves. These same trumpets are also used to frighten any enemies.

Chapter 4: The Olympians

They are the most recognizable figures in Greek Mythology, whose influence can still be seen even in modern literature. The twelve major gods of Ancient Greece presided over all aspects of human life. They were revered, worshipped, and many even have temples dedicated to them. Some of which have survived the test of time, and can still be visited today. Though their temples may lie in ruins, the lore behind these figures is still some of the finest and most complex in history.

There are major gods (the Olympians) and minor gods in the Greek Pantheon. The minor gods served as minions for the twelve. For example, the muses belonged to Apollo, the Horae belonged to Zeus, the Erotes belonged to Aphrodite, and the Eileithyia belonged to both Hera and Hebe.

The Different Categories of Olympian Gods

Theoi Agoraioi – These were the gods of the "agora", also known as the assembly and marketplace. Zeus, who is considered to be the god of all kings and princes, governed over the assembly. He did so together with Athena, the goddess of wise counsel, Themis (Custom), Dike (Justice), and Calliope (Eloquence).

The marketplace, on the other hand, was presided over by the god of commerce, Hermes. Along with Hephaestus and Athena, both of whom are considered to be patron gods of artisans (the potters, the weavers, sculptors, metalworkers, and so on). Apollo is often associated with the marketplace as well, though he is not quite as popular as the previously mentioned gods.

Theoi Daitoi – They were the gods of the different banquets and feasts. Included here are Dionysus, who is best known as the god of wine, and Hestia, the goddess of the feasts. Other festive gods such as Aphrodite, the goddess of pleasure, and the Charites, the goddesses of dancing, joy and other amusements often joined them in revelry as well. The Theoi Mousikoi, the gods of music, also partook in these feasts.

Theoi Gamelioi – These gods presided over marriages. The main gods who dealt with these were Zeus, Hera, and Aphrodite. However, they were also joined by minor gods such as the Erotes (loves), Hymenaios (wedding song), Peitho (persuasion), Harmonia (harmony), the Charites (graces), Hebe (youth), and Eunomia (good order).

Theoi Georgikoi – They were the gods of agriculture. Demeter was at the top of their list, but they were mainly comprised of chthonic gods who were non-Olympian.

Theoi Gymnastikoi – These were the gods of the gymnasium, of the games, and of athletics. Ranked among them are Hermes, Nike, Heracles and the Dioscuri, and Agon. Eros, often referred to as the god of comradeship, was also worshipped in the gymnasia.

Theoi Halioi – Their king, Poseidon, led the gods of the sea. There are also other Olympian gods who had maritime roles, among them, are Artemis, Apollo, Aphrodite, and the Dioscuri. They presided over safe voyage, embarkations, salvation from storms, and the harbors. Many of the gods who fall into this category were non-Olympian and were considered to be minor divinities

Theoi Iatrikoi – These were the gods of healing and medicine. They belonged to Apollo's entourage, and included among their number is his son, the medicine-god Asclepius and his family: Hygeia (good health), Epione (soothing), Aegle (radiance), Panaceia (curative), Iaso (healing), Telesphorus (accomplished), and Aceso (cure).

Theoi Ktesioi – The gods of house and home. Zeus, the protector of the home and family courtyard was first in their list. Hestia, the goddess of the heart was also included. Other household gods such as Hermes and Hecate were part of this group, as they protected the different entranceways to a home.

Theoi Mantikoi – These were the gods of oracles, prophecy, and divination. At their head was Apollo, who is known as the god of seers and oracles, as well as by Zeus, who is the god of fate. There are other oracular gods who are included in this group. They are the Titanesses Phoebe (known as the oracle of Delphi), Themis (in both Delphi and Dodona), Mnemosyne (in Lebadeia) and Dione (in Dodona). The god Hermes also presided over a number of primitive varieties of divination, including coin-throwing oracles, casting of stones, and even in Astrology.

Theoi Nomioi – These were the gods of the countryside, as well as of different country pursuits. Among the activities included are fishing, fowling, hunting, and the herding of cattle. At their heart are the Olympians Hermes (for herding), Artemis (for hunting), and the wine-god Dionysus. The rest of their entourage was comprised of rustic, non-Olympian divinities.

Theoi Mousikoi – These were the known gods of music, the arts, and dance. The Olympian twin gods Artemis and Apollo took center stage for this group. Apollo presided over poetry and music, whilst Artemis presided over the dances and choirs of girls. The other important gods included in this group are the nine Muses, the dancing Graces or Charites, and the musical demigods in the form of Linos and Hymenaeus. Hermes, Dionysus, and Aphrodite were also associated with music and the arts.

Theoi Polemikoi – The intimidating gods of war. The mighty Athena and Ares were the considered the focal points of power for this group. Included were the minor gods in the form of Enyo, Nike, Eris, Deimos, and Phobos. Zeus and Apollo were also associated with this group, as both had wartime functions.

Theoi Thesmioi – These were the gods of custom and divine law. Zeus and Demeter were at the top of the Thesmioi. The minor gods who were also included in this group included the Horae— specifically, Dike, Irene, Eunomia, Themis, and Apollo.

The Major Olympian Gods and Goddesses

ZEUS (Ζευς)

The King of the Gods, who was also the god of the sky, of the weather, of destiny, fate, as well as law and order. He is also associated with kingship.

In art, he is depicted as a mature man, regal in stature, and he often carried a royal scepter and a fearsome lightning bolt. In these depictions, an eagle also often accompanied him.

Family:

- He is the youngest son of the Titans, Cronos, and Rhea.

- He's also the youngest brother of the gods Hades, Poseidon, Hestia, Hera, and Demeter.

- Husband to the sky-goddess Hera, they had three offspring: Hebe, Ares, and Eileithyia. Their union is tumultuous, and this is often attributed to Zeus and his womanizing ways. In fact, he has fathered innumerable mortal kings as well as heroes; the most famous of which include: Helen of Troy, Heracles, and Perseus.

Associations:

- Aside from Hera, he also had other divine consorts. Demeter, the mother of Persephone. His cousin Metis, who is the mother of Athena. Maia, the mother of Hermes. Leto, the mother of Apollo. His aunts Themis, the mother of the Moirai (the Fates) and Dione, the mother of Aphrodite. He also consorted with Mnemosyne, the mother of the Muses, and with his descendant Semele, who is the more of Dionysus.

- In some texts, it is said that the early generations of men succumbed to corruption and wickedness, prompting Zeus to wipe them out through a great deluge. In this catastrophe, only a virtuous pair were spared. Deukalion and Pyrrha were given the task of repopulating the earth by casting varied stones, which later transformed into men.

- Zeus is also known to have seduced many mortal women and as such, producing numerous demigods. He seduced Leda under the guise of a swan, Danae as a shower of gold, Europa as a bull, and Alcmene by using the guise of her own husband, Callisto after he transformed into the likeness of Artemis, and Antiope as a satyr.

- Among his many mortal offspring, Zeus favored Heracles the most. In fact, the god supported him through various trials and was also welcomed into Olympus as a god.

- As most gods were, Zeus was also wrathful and served punishment to some of the worst villains in mythology for their deeds. These included: Lycaon which served human flesh to the gods, Tantalos who took ambrosia from the heavens, Ixion who tried to rape Hera, and lastly, Salmoneus who took upon the identity of the god in attempt to steal the worship which was due to him.

As King of the Gods, Zeus had quite the significant retinue and was often accompanied by many lesser divinities. For example, his throne was known to have been guarded by four different winged spirits:

- *Kratos (Strength)*

- *Nike (Victory)*

- *Zelos (Rivalry)*

- *Bia (Force)*

Kratos and Bia were the enforcers, often tasked with jobs such as apprehension of those who have offended the gods, or the imprisonment of those who oppose them. Nike drove his chariot, often accompanying the god in miniature form as something akin to a familiar.

Then we have Hermes who served as his personal herald; acting as envoy, diplomat and general agent of his will. His messenger, however, was Iris. Also known as the winged goddess of the rainbow, she relayed messages and delivered various commands from Zeus to the other gods.

Themis was his high councilor and she sat beside his throne. Themis had her own attendants—the six daughters of the Moirai (Fates) and the Horai (Seasons). This collective was responsible for keeping the cosmos functioning properly. Themis was also tasked with calling upon all of the gods in the courtyard during various assemblies.

When it comes to his more unusual attendants, Metis certainly tops this list. You may recall that Zeus swallowed her whole in order to avoid the prophecy that her son would be the end of his reign. In swallowing Metis, he also implanted her wise counsel in his mind. Do note that Ancient Greeks believed the belly to be the seat of emotion and thought, instead of the brain.

Metis continued to exist in some form within Zeus, even retaining the ability to give birth to Athena, and equipping her with armor as well as weaponry before her second birth through the top of his head.

Hebe and Ganymede were both cupbearers for Zeus and they would serve him nectar as well as Ambrosia during the feasts of the gods. The Harpies, also known as "The Hounds of Zeus" were rather crude creatures who were tasked with carrying off or harassing any mortal the god would put them to.

Lastly, and this is a mythological creature many would be familiar with, we have his winged-horse Pegasus. He carried the god's many lightning bolts and drew his chariot across the heavens.

POSEIDON (Ποσειδῶν)

Poseidon is the Olympian god of the sea, of floods, of earthquakes, drought, and horses. Like Zeus, he is often depicted as a mature man of sturdy built, and a dark beard.

He is also commonly pictured holding a Trident (a three-pronged spear used by fishermen) that has become the symbol most associated with him.

Family:

- He is the son of the Titans, Cronos, and Rhea. However, unlike his brother Zeus, Poseidon was among his siblings who were swallowed whole by their father. They were later rescued by the youngest of the brood and after defeating their father and the other Titans; he reigned with his brother and sisters from Mount Olympus.

- Poseidon married the sea-goddess Amphitrite who is Nereus' eldest child. This is a marital alliance, which also helped secure the god's dominion over the sea. Poseidon and Amphitrite had a son together, the fishtailed god Triton.

- However, much like Zeus, Poseidon also had a number of mortal offspring such as the Cyclops Polyphemos and the giant Antaios. He is also father to the magical horses Pegasus and Arion.

- Poseidon also had human offspring, and many of them became kings. However, the most recognizable are Theseus and Bellerophontes.

Associations:

- Poseidon's sacred animals were the dolphin, the horse, and the bull. As god of the sea, he is also often associated with various marine creatures. The most famous of which would be the Cretan Bull, sire of the legendary Minotaur.

- A pair of Hippokampoi or fishtailed horses drew his chariot.

- His sacred plants were the wild celery and the pine tree, pieces of which were used to crown the victors at the god's Isthmian Games.

With Poseidon's story, we must begin at the moment of his birth when his mother Rhea attempted to hide him among a flock of lambs. Most people would know of Zeus' story, but not of Poseidon's. Instead of handing him over to his father, Rhea brought the Titan king a young horse instead— which Cronos promptly devoured. However, this plan, though successful at first, wasn't to last long. His father did discover him eventually, and like his siblings before him, he too was swallowed whole.

In some texts, Poseidon is often described as being an equal with Zeus when it came to dignity, but weaker in terms of power. The youngest lords this fact over him, even prompting Poseidon to conspire with Hera to put him in chains. For the most part, however, he is much humbler and we often read about him yielding to the King of the gods.

As the god ruler of the sea, Poseidon is said to have the power to call forth storms and gather clouds, creating tumultuous seas for any seafarer who may have offended him. At the same time, he is known to grant safe voyage, as well as rescue those who are in danger. Given that the sea wraps around the entire earth, Poseidon is also often referred to as "***The God who holds the Earth***".

HERMES (Ἑρμῆς)

Hermes was the Olympian god of travelers and hospitality, but he also ruled a number of other aspects of daily life. For example, he was also known as the god of flocks and herds, of astrology and astronomy, of cunning and thievery, of language and writing, of heralds and diplomacy, of gymnasiums and contests, as well as of roads and trade.

He is also part of Zeus's retinue, as the god's personal messenger and herald. In some texts, Hermes is also shown to be the guide of those who have departed this life, leading their souls down into the underworld.

Unlike Zeus and Poseidon who were often shown to be older men, Hermes is depicted as a handsome youth who wore winged boots and carried around a herald's wand.

Family:

- He is the son of Zeus and of the Pleiad-nymphai, Maia. This makes him the grandson of the Titans Cronos and Rhea, as well as that of Atlas and the nymphai, Pleione.

- He has a number of half-brothers and sisters, which includes many Olympian gods such as Artemis, Apollo, Athena, Persephone, Dionysus, and Ares.

- He is the second youngest out of the twelve Olympian gods, which is also why he is often depicted as a beardless youth.

- Hermes fathered the goat-legged god Pan by the nymphai Penelopeia. Aside from Pan, he also had a number of mortal offspring.

Associations:

- Hermes' sacred animals are the hare and the ram. In some art, he is even depicted to be riding on the back of a large ram. Given that he is god of the herd, he is also associated with sheep, goats, and cattle.

- His sacred plants are the strawberry tree and the crocus flower.

- Hermes' most distinctive attribute would be the herald's wand, but in some depictions, he is shown to be carrying a short sword instead.

- Another item that is closely associated with the god would be his winged boots and helmet. In some cases, the helmet would be drawn with wings as well. This is a nod to his role as messenger, signifying his swiftness.

- Another unique symbol that Hermes is known for would be the "Herma" or a stone road-marker that also often doubles as a wayside shrine. Most primitive Hermae were made out of standing stones, whilst the more elaborate ones were carved with the head of a god, or the herald's wand symbol.

Winged Boots and Helmet:

- There's more to Hermes' winged boots and winged helmet than just being perceived as a mere costume. In fact, his leather boots were often referred to by the Ancient Greeks as "pteroeis pedila". It provided him with great speed, allowing the god to accomplish his duties fully and efficiently.

- His helmet sometimes depicted a wide-brimmed hat, was actually the hat of Aidoneus. Also known as "The Unseen", Aidoneus' hat provided Hermes' with the ability to be stealthier as it rendered him invisible to the naked eye.

Some people liken Hermes to the trickster god Loki of Norse Mythology, and this is done with good reason. In many texts, it is said that as a newborn infant, Hermes snuck out of his crib and actually stole Apollo's cattle. At the same time, he also fashioned a lyre out of a tortoise-shell. Zeus, amused by his son's antics, provided him with a seat among the Olympians.

Endowed with shrewdness, Hermes is also said to have many inventions aside from the lyre. In fact, he is said to have been the author of astronomy, of the alphabet, of music, of numbers, and of the art of fighting. Texts also say that he first mastered the cultivation of the olive tree, of weights and measures, and many other things. *(Plut. Sympos. ix. 3; Diod. l.c. and v. 75; Hygin. Fab. 277.)*

HERA (Ἥρη)

Hera is known as the Queen of the gods and as Zeus' consort. She reigns over women, marriage, the heavens—including the sky and the stars.

In her many depictions, Hera is usually shown as a beautiful woman who wore a crown atop her head and held a royal scepter with a lotus tip.

In some depictions, a hawk, a cuckoo or a lion accompanies her.

Family:

- There is some debate as to whether Hera is the eldest daughter of Cronos and Rhea, however, she is among the first siblings who were swallowed whole by their Titan father. In some texts, she is even referred to as Zeus' twin sister, though there isn't much to supplement this.

- According to Homeric poems, Thetys and Oceanus raised Hera—her marriage with Zeus was, in fact, unknown to both her parents.

- After her marriage with Zeus, she became just as revered by her husband. In fact, Zeus, himself, was known to listen to her counsel and even spoke to her about his many secrets instead of seeking the ear of other gods.

- In terms of power, she is inferior to him and is obligated to be submissive to him like the other gods are. He status as his consort does not exempt Hera from getting chastised by Zeus should she ever commit an offense against him.

- By Zeus, she is mother to Hebe, Hephaestus, and Ares.

Character:

- As described by Homer, Hera isn't the most amiable goddess. In fact, her main character features are obstinacy, jealousy, and a predisposition for vengeance. She can become so fearsome that it is said Hera can make her own husband tremble.

- She is also known to persecute her husband's many mistresses in rather harsh ways—such is the case with Semele, Leto, and Alcmene. It is these stories that have given her the reputation of being cruel and vengeful.

- That said, Hera can be quite amiable as well—a good example of which was her assistance of the Argonauts during their quest for the golden fleece. The group's leader, Jason, was among her favorites. Hera is also known to have assisted the Greeks during the Trojan War

Marriage with Zeus:

- Hera is known to be the only married goddess.

- As the story goes, it was during her maidenhood that first fell in love with the goddess. Going as far as changing himself into a cuckoo bird in order to seduce her.

- Eventually, Hera grew up to be the most beautiful of all the goddesses and Zeus, despite their common blood, made her his bride. It must be noted that marriages between gods, despite familial ties, isn't at all uncommon.

- As wedding present, Gaia (the Earth) created for her the famed garden of the golden apples. This is where Hesperides and the Dragon Ladon stood guard.

Despite her reputation for being vengeful and cruel towards those who offend her, the Ancient Greeks still built many sanctuaries for the goddess. She was also worshipped in many parts of Greece, sometimes in common with Zeus. This could be attributed to the fact that she represented many other things, symbolizing the sanctity of marriage as well as women.

In some cases, she was also regarded as personification of the atmosphere, as well as queen of both heavens and stars.

DEMETER (Δημητηρ)

Demeter is the goddess of agriculture, bread, and grain. She helped sustain mankind with all the bounties of the Earth.

Demeter also presided over the Mystery Cults, the very same ones that promised their initiates a path to a blessed afterlife in Elysium.

In depictions, Demeter is often shown as a mature woman wearing a crown, which bore a cornucopia or sheaves of wheat, along with a torch.

Family:

- Demeter is a daughter of the Titans Cronos and Rhea. Much like her other siblings, she too was devoured whole by their father, before being rescued by Zeus.

- She is mother to Dionysus and Persephone, both of whom was fathered by Zeus. She is also mother to a divine creature, the horse Arion, by Poseidon of Despoena.

Associations:

- The most commonly associated symbols with her are the cornucopia and the sheaf of grain she is often depicted with.

- Her sacred animals are the snake and the pig.

- Her sacred plants are poppies, mint, and wheat.

- When it comes to her retinue, it is often said that Hecate, Plutus, Iacchus, and Triptolemus accompany Demeter.

Unlike Hera, Demeter is often described to be amiable—motherly in every sense of the word. She fed mankind and made sure that their harvests are plentiful. In fact, one particular story tells of the journey of Triptolemos, a hero who was sent forth by the goddess to provide mankind with knowledge on agriculture.

Demeter and her daughter, Persephone

Arguably, the most prominent mythos that Demeter is associated with would be the abduction of her daughter Persephone by Hades. As the story goes, Demeter was unaware that Zeus had promised their daughter to Hades.

Whilst the young maiden was gathering flowers one day, flowers which Zeus himself had caused to bloom to favor Hades' scheme, the earth opened up and she was carried away into the underworld by the god. Helios and Hecate heard her cries, while Demeter merely heard echoes of it—but they were enough to prompt her to begin the search for her daughter.

For nine days, the goddess wandered the earth, neglecting to take ambrosia or nectar. On the tenth, she met with Hecate who informed her that she had heard Persephone's cries but knew not who had taken the young goddess. Both then went to Helios who informed them that it was Hades who had taken her daughter and that it was done with the consent of Zeus.

In her anger upon learning this, Demeter avoided Olympus and resided among mankind. Providing them with blessings wherever she was received kindly, and punishing those who did not receive her gifts with the proper reverence. In time, she also put famine upon the earth, leaving Zeus anxious over the fate of the mortals. It is then that he sent Iris to try and induce the goddess to return home.

This was to be in vain, however. Demeter vowed to never restore fertility on earth until she meets with her daughter again.

HEPHAESTUS (Ήφαιστος)

He was known as the Olympian god of smiths, of fire, craftsmen, stonemasonry, metalworking, and of sculpture.

Hephaestus was often depicted as a bearded man riding a donkey, and he often held the tools of a smith: hammer and tongs.

Hephaestus was known as the god's forger and his skill was incomparable, even among the deities. He alone possessed this talent, making him indispensable to the Olympians.

Family:

- Contrary to what most people would think, he was born of Hera alone, though some texts refer to him as Zeus' son. He was birthed from Hera's thigh and his parentage was kept secret from him until he managed to get the answer from his own mother.

- Hephaestus was also present during the birth of Athena, helping to split open Zeus' head in order to set the young goddess free.

- His consort was Aphrodite, though some texts also mention Charis Aglaea as being his wife.

- He has a number of immortal children, including the Kabeiroi the Palikoi, Thaleia, and Kadmilos. Along with his immortal children, he also had plenty of mortal offspring—many of whom became kings.

Associations:

- He is best known as the god of fire and volcanic districts in Ancient Greece often revered him. He is also god to the smiths and metalworkers.

- His symbols are the hammer and tongs, whilst his sacred animal is the hardworking donkey.

- His retinue is comprised of Cyclopes and Celedones.

Hephaestus differs from other gods in such a way that, unlike them, he is shown to have a disability—he has weak legs and therefore, wobbles his way along. That said, his chest and upper body are muscular and strong, allowing him to work as much as he does.

The source of his disability varies when it comes to text, but the general consensus in mythology is that he was born in that way

(Homeric texts). However, some suggest that he sustained this disability after having been thrown from Olympus by his mother or Zeus. Eventually, and after sending up a golden chair that trapped Hera in her seat, he was asked to return and be the smith for the Olympians.

It must also be noted that he was given his own palace in Olympus. One that shone like stars and was imperishable. In it were his workshop, twenty bellows (which worked according to his bidding), and his anvil. This is where all of his creations, both for gods and men, were forged.

He is also often compared to Athena in that, like her, he gave his skill to mortal artists.

DIONYSUS (Διονυσος)

He was the Olympian god of wine, pleasure, madness, festivity, vegetation, and wild frenzy. Dionysus is often depicted in two different ways; some showed him as an older, bearded god whilst there are others who portrayed him as a feminine, longhaired youth.

His main attributes include the thyrsus or a pinecone-tipped staff, a crown of ivy, and a drinking cup. The Maenads and a troop of Satyrs also often accompany him.

Family:

- Dionysus is the son of Zeus and Princess Semele of Thebes. However, during her pregnancy, Hera who was jealous because of her husband's adulterous ways, tricked the princess into requesting to see Zeus' full form. As he is bound by oath, the god had no choice but to comply, subsequently incinerating Semele with the heat of his lightning bolts. From her body, he recovered their unborn child and sewed him onto his thigh. Zeus carried Dionysus to term in this manner.

- Dionysus' consort is Ariadne, who is the daughter of Minos and Pasiphae of Creta. She is best known for helping Theseus escape the Labyrinth.

- With Ariadne, Dionysus fathered Thoas, Oenopion, Staphylos, and Peparethos.

Associations:

- Dionysus' sacred animals are the serpent, tiger, and bull. The god is also often depicted to be riding on the back of a panther or driving a chariot drawn by a pair of the same beasts.

- His sacred plants include bindweed, ivy, the grapevine, and the pine tree. His devotees also often wore wreaths of ivy and carried with them pinecone tipped staffs.

- His retinue is comprised of Silenus, the Maenads, and the Satyrs.

Most people would immediately associate Dionysus with wine and revelry—of madness—but few really know why he's considered to be the god of this particular human aspect. To better understand this, we must return to the time he reached adulthood, the same moment at which Hera inflicted this madness upon him. It is said that after this fact, Dionysus began to wander through Syria and Egypt where the Egyptian King, Proteus, welcomed him. It must also be noted that he was eventually cured of this madness, but his travels continued on and later brought him to Asia.

As god of wine, he is both an inspired and inspiring god—Dionysus had the power to reveal the future through oracles. Despite often being portrayed as being the center of chaotic feasts, the god was also characterized as being a lawgiver and a lover of peace.

ATHENA (Αθηνη)

Athena was the Olympian goddess of war and the defense of towns, she was also known as the goddess of good counsel and wisdom, of heroic endeavor, of pottery, weaving, and various other crafts.

She was often depicted as armed with a spear and a shield and adorned with a crested helm. Athena was also typically shown wearing a long robe whilst bearing the Aegis, a cape trimmed with snakes that also displays the features of the fearsome Gorgon, Medusa.

Family:

- Athena is the daughter of Zeus and his first wife, Metis. As the story goes, fearing the prophecy left by Gaia and Cronos, Zeus swallowed Metis whole while she was pregnant with Athena. Inside the god, Metis gave birth to their daughter. She sprang forth from her father's head in full armor, and in some texts, it is also said that instead of a loud cry, Athena gave a war-shout instead.

- Unlike most of her siblings, Athena remained a virgin goddess and mothered no offspring. However, she did adopt Erikthonios as her own son, following the attempted violation upon her made by Hephaestus. It is said that the god spilled his seed upon the earth and produced Erikthonios.

Associations:

- Athena's symbols included the Gorgoneion and the Aegis. Her sacred animal is the owl, often thought to symbolize the goddess' wisdom. Her sacred plant is the Olive tree.

- Aside from wisdom, war, and her skill for war strategy, Athena is also commonly associated with crafts and weaving. A skill that she gifted mankind with.

- When it comes to her retinue, Athena has the least amount of people, having only Nike (Victory) to accompany her.

Athena is, arguably, one of the most worshipped goddesses among the Olympians and this comes as no surprise. It is believed that she invented nearly all of the work in which women were employed, and is often compared to Hephaestus when it comes to skill in craftsmanship. It is only later that she also came to be regarded as goddess of art, knowledge, and wisdom—often depicted being seated at the right hand of her father and providing him with counsel.

As her name might suggest, Athena was also patron divinity of the state. In fact, she was at Athens with the responsibility of looking after the phratries and houses, which formed the very basis of said state. Athena also maintained justice, the authority of law, and of order within the courts and assembly of people. Athena was worshipped in all of Greece.

Among the gods and goddesses, she was also one of the few who is mentioned in countless myths. We recall a few of them below:

I.   Athena and the Gorgon, Medusa:

It is said, that before turning into the monstrous creature most people know of her as, Medusa was, in fact, a famed beauty. She had many suitors and of her many charming attributes, it was her hair that people found to be the loveliest.

According to text, Medusa was violated by Poseidon in one of Athena's shrines. However, the goddess turned away from her and covered her virgin eyes with the shield she held. Athena saw this incident as an offense towards her and as punishment; she transformed Medusa's hair into terrible snakes.

II.   Athena and Arachne:

Many mortal beings tend to incur the wrath of the gods through hubris—that is, claiming that they were far superior to them in some capacity. Such is the case with Arachne, who believed her own skill at wool-craft to far surpass that of the goddess'. It is said that to watch her work, even the Nymphae would leave their stead, enamored by the young maiden's grace. Many believed her to be trained by Athena, but the girl denied that her gifts were God-given, a blasphemy in the eyes of the goddess.

To challenge Arachne, Athena changed her form into that of an old woman, offering advice and telling her to ask pardon for the blasphemous words she had let spill. However, Arachne did not heed any of these—shouting at the top of her lungs at the disguised Athena to leave and furthering her offense. At this, the goddess threw off her disguise, making the Lydian women and even the Nymphae bend the knee in reverence. Arachne did not show the same devotion, however.

Though Arachne's skill was of true magnificence, it was her hubris that was to become her downfall. In the end, the goddess turned her into a small creature that hung along doorways, weaving its own silk endlessly—Arachne became the first spider.

APHRODITE (Αφροδιτη)

Aphrodite was the Olympian goddess of beauty, love, procreation, and pleasure.

In her many different depictions, she is often shown as a beautiful woman who was accompanied by the winged god-ling Eros.

Another common attribute between depictions of the goddess is the fact that she's often shown in the nude—this can be seen in both frescoes and classical sculptures.

Family:

- When it comes to her birth, there are two different texts that are usually mentioned. The first of which is her birth through the sea foam, which gathered around the mutilated genitals of Uranus. However, the most accepted is that she is a daughter of Zeus through Dione.

- Aphrodite, being the goddess of procreation, bore many immortal offspring. The most commonly known of which would be Eros. She also mothered Deimos, Harmonia, and Phobos by Ares. As well as Priapos and Iakkhos by Dionysus.

- Her primary consort is Hephaestus, but her adulterous affair with the war-god Ares is a significant part of her mythology. Aside from him, Aphrodite also had many other lovers.

Associations:

- Aphrodite symbolized beauty in many different aspects and she was associated with many aspects of being a woman as well. Her symbols included the godling, Eros, and the conch shell. Among her sacred animals are the dove and the goose. As for her sacred plants, Aphrodite had two: the rose and the myrtle.

- Included in her retinue are the Charites, the Erotes, Peitho, and Eros.

Though she is considered to be the goddess of love, mythology talks plenty of the instances in which Aphrodite punished those who offended her rather harshly. At the same time, however, those she favored received her blessings and protection.

She is beautiful and graceful, surpassing all of the other goddesses, and receiving the price of beauty from Paris. As such, during the Trojan war, it is said that she sided with the Trojans, and even saved Paris during his duel with Menelaus.

However, when she sought to help her mortal son Aeneas in the same war, Diomedes hindered her from doing so. This frightened the goddess so much that she left her son and was carried off by Iris back to Olympus where she complained of the misfortune to her mother, Dione.

I.   Aphrodite and her Lovers

Though she was married to Hephaestus, Aphrodite was an unfaithful wife and carried on numerous affairs with other gods and even mortal men alike. Her affair with Ares is the subject of many myths. However, he is not the only god who was charmed by the goddess. She also favored Hermes, Dionysus, and even Poseidon.

Aphrodite is known for her mischief as well, often kindling love in the hearts of gods for their mortal subjects. Zeus did not let this go unpunished, of course, and gave the goddess a taste of her own medicine. Within her, he inspired a passion for Anchises, a mortal man, and with whom she had Lynus and Aeneas.

ARES (Αρης)

Ares is best known as the Olympian god of battle lust, war, courage and civil order.

In numerous Grecian art, he is often depicted as a bearded warrior who is fully dressed in armor.

However, there are also instances where he is pictured as a youth, dressed in nothing save for his helm, and the spear in his hand.

Among the gods, he is also known to have the worst of tempers and is often characterized as angry, and a bit of a brute.

Family:

- Ares is the son of Zeus and Hera and is the eldest brother of the goddesses Hebe and Eileithyia. He is also the half-brother of Athena, Artemis, Apollo, Aphrodite, Dionysus, and Hephaestus.

- With Aphrodite, he had three children: Deimos, Phobos, and Harmiona. Harmonia's daughter, Semele, was also the mother of the god Dionysus.

- Like his siblings, Ares also fathered a number of mortal offspring and many of them inherited his rather violent temperament. In fact, unlike the other demigods who were often characterized as heroes, Ares' mortal sons were often depicted as villains.

Associations:

- Ares' symbol is the helm and he is often depicted wearing one. His sacred animal is the serpent, and there are no known sacred plants associated with him.

- In depictions where he is featured with the other gods, such as during feasts, he is often seen with his helm off and carried in his hand. Among his other attributes are the shield, a sheathed sword, and a spear.

- Much like Athena, he is also shown wearing armor. This includes a short tunic, greaves, his helm, and breastplate.

- Aside from the serpent, he is also sometimes associated with the vulture and some species, particularly predatory ones, of owls.

- As for his retinue, it is fitting that he is accompanied by some fearsome divine beings including Enyo, Deimos, and Phobos.

Ares, unlike Athena who represents wisdom and strategy when it comes to war, is often regarded as the personification of strength and boldness. It is his sister Eris who calls forth war while Zeus directs the very course it follows. Ares, on the other hand, loves war for all its chaos—the noise, the slaughter of soldiers and civilians, and even in the destruction of towns in the process. When Ancient Greeks thought of Ares, it is savagery that comes to mind.

It is this attitude and mentality that made him an outsider when it comes to his parents and other gods. Instead, he is surrounded by all the terrible personifications of war such as Fear and Strife. This being said, Ares is not always victorious when it comes to his conquests. Despite his great physical strength, he is often conquered when faced with a higher power—such as the case with Diomedes who was assisted by his sister, Athena.

The Ancient Greeks believed that the warlike character of Thrace's tribes was due to the fact that the god had taken up residence there. It is there and in Scythia where the principal places of worship to Ares can be found.

APOLLO (Απολλων)

Apollo was the Olympian god of music, poetry, and song. He is also associated with oracles and prophecy. In later texts, they also associated him with healing, archery, disease, plague, and the protection of youth.

In depictions, he is often shown as a young, handsome man. Beardless, but he was shown having long hair.

The most common attributes that accompanied him were a branch of laurel, a wreath, a bow and quiver, a lyre, and a raven.

Family:

- Apollo is the son of Zeus and Leto. He is also the twin brother of Artemis. During the birth of the twin gods, their mother was assisted by all of the goddesses, save for Hera and Eileithyia. However, the latter did rush to Leto's aid as soon as she learned of what was unfolding.

- Apollo has a number of divine offspring from different mothers. His offspring include Aristaios (by Kyrene), Asklepios (by Koronis), Khariklo, Korybantes Samothrakiai (these daimones were said to be borne of Apollo and the nymph Rhetia, though some texts suggest that their mother was the muse, Thaleia). He also had many mortal offspring; some even possessed his ability as a seer.

Associations:

- Apollo's symbols were the bow and the lyre. He was often depicted as carrying one or both of these items. His sacred animals are the raven and the swan, whilst his sacred plants include the laurel, the cypress, and the larkspur.

- His retinue befits his title as god of music, poetry, and song. It is comprised of the muses, offering inspiration to both the god and those devoted to him.

Apollo and Daphne

Among the many myths about Apollo, the one about the naiad, Daphne stands out the most. As the story goes, she was beloved by the God who continued to pursue her until she grew exhausted from the chase and cried out to Gaia for help. Gaia, heeding the naiad's call, transformed her into a laurel tree. Apollo, still in love with Daphne, and broken over his loss, adopted the tree as his sacred plant.

I.   Apollo, the God Who Punishes and Destroys

His skill with the bow has been written in many texts and hymns, all recounting stories about how his arrows never miss a target despite great distances. In some cases, the sudden deaths of men were believed to be the consequence of his arrows. It is with these same arrows that he is said to have brought upon the plague into the Grecian camp. Ancient Greeks also related his name "Apollo" to Apollumi, which means, "to destroy".

II.   Apollo, the God of Prophecy

We're most familiar with Apollo delighting and entertaining both the Olympians, as well as other divine creatures with his music. However, few also know of the fact that he has power over a number of oracles, particularly of the one found in Delphi. He had the ability to communicate this power to both the gods, as well as men, and many ancient seers are associated with him in some capacity.

ARTEMIS (Αρτεμις)

Artemis was known as the Olympian goddess of the wilderness, of wild animals, and of hunting. She is also recognized as the goddess of childbirth, and the protector of girls from birth until the age of marriage. This is in companion with her brother being the protector of young boys from the same age.

Together, Artemis and Apollo were also seen as the bringers of disease and sudden death. In the same manner, it was said that Artemis targeted the women and young girls, whilst Apollo the men and young boys.

In most, if not all, of her depictions, Artemis was typically shown as a young maiden or girl who held a hunting bow and a quiver of arrows.

Family:

- Artemis is the daughter of Zeus and the Titaness, Leto. She is also the twin sister of the god Apollo. She is also the granddaughter of four elder Titans: Cronos, Rhea, Phoibe, and Koios. She is half-sister to many Olympian gods as well.

- Much like Athena, the goddess bore no children. However, as a virgin goddess, Artemis was often portrayed as girl-woman rather than as a fully-grown adult woman.

Associations:

- Artemis' most recognizable attributes would have to be the bow and arrows she is always seen carrying. However, these aren't the only weapons she is depicted as having. The goddess is sometimes equipped with a pair of hunting spears, a torch, a water jug, and a quiver.

- She was also often clothed in a girl's dress that's knee-length or one that is full-length. As she is often hunting, the goddess always wears a cloak over this and has a headgear to top it all off. In some depictions, she is shown wearing the pelt of a deer draped across her shoulders.

- Artemis' sacred animal is the deer and it is said that she drove a chariot that is pulled by a pair of the beasts. Sometimes she is also pictured during or after the hunt, sometimes holding or chasing after one of the creatures.

- The golden-horned Cerynitian Hind is one of her most celebrated sacred animals. She is also associated with the bear, with ground birds such as partridges, guinea fowl, and quails.

- Her sacred plants are the palm tree and the cypress tree.

Artemis is one of the most familiar names you'll hear when it comes to the Olympians. There's a plenty of different myths about her, and you'll find that she is almost never without her brother in them. Like Apollo, there is some duality when it comes to what the goddess represents. For example, she is known to be a *"thea appollousa"* or someone who sends death and plague to mankind.

At the same time, she is also a *"thea soteira"* which basically means that she is capable of curing and alleviating man's sufferings. A good example of which was when she healed Aeneas after he was carried into the temple of her brother. That said, there isn't much similarity between the twin gods. In fact, Apollo is often identified with the sun whilst Artemis is identified with the moon.

In worship, she is known to be the protector of young girls as well as young animals. This includes the wild game that roamed the mountains and the forests. The priestesses and priests who were devoted to her were all bound to live chastely, much like the goddess herself. She is also known to be a protector of the nymphs.

HADES (Ἀιδης)

Hades was the god of the dead and the king of the underworld. He is the god who ruled over funeral rites.

He is also known as god of the earth's hidden wealth, starting from the fertile soil that nourishes the seeds, to the mined earth that provides gold, silver, and other precious metals.

He is often depicted as a regal looking man, dark-haired and bearded. Hades is also often shown holding a bird-tipped scepter whilst seated upon his throne in the underworld.

Family:

- He is the son of Cronos and Rhea. Much like his other siblings, he too was swallowed whole by their father and was later rescued by Zeus.

- He is Persephone's consort and as the myth goes, this arrangement is one that happens by force.

- By Persephone, he fathered the Erinyes and Melinoe. He is also father to Makaria and Zagreus.

Associations:

- His symbols include the royal scepter and the cornucopia. His sacred animal is the screech owl, and his sacred plants are white poplar, mint, and asphodel.

- His retinue is comprised of the Erinyes, the judges of the dead, and the three-headed dog Cerberus.

Hades came to reign in the darkness of the underworld after he drew lots with his two other brothers. Zeus received the heavens and his other brother, Poseidon, received the sea. The earth and Olympus do belong to all three and he has the option to ascend anytime he wishes.

His character is often described as being rather fierce and in some cases; he is the most hated by mortal men out of all the gods. In fact, whenever sacrifices are made to him and Persephone, it would consist of a pair of male and female sheep, both colored black. The person who was tasked to make the sacrifice had to turn their face away whilst doing so.

The Abduction and Return of Persephone:

To continue from Demeter's perspective of the story, we now find ourselves deep in the belly of the underworld where Hades dwelt, and the same place where he had taken Persephone. By this time, the earth has been suffering from the drought that Demeter had unleashed upon it and Zeus is desperate to appease her—to prevent the destruction of mortal men.

As such, he sent Hermes to Erebus to speak to Hades and lead Persephone out of the realm. The messenger god found Persephone seated with her husband, brooding over her ill-fate. When Hades concedes to Zeus' request to free her, she does liven up and followed Hermes back to the mortal upon his chariot.

However, Hades was not sending her back to her mother with no strings attached. Unbeknownst to them, he had secretly given her sweet pomegranate seeds to eat, thus ensuring that he would have to go back to her. Because she had tasted of food from the land of the dead, Persephone is now bound to return to Hades' realm for a third part of the seasons every year.

And this is why we have the changing of seasons. When the earth is full of life and color, we know that Persephone is back with her mother. During the times that it is gloomy and barren, we know that she is grieving her daughter's return to Hades.

Chapter 5: Of Monsters and Heroes

In Greek Mythology, there are many fearsome monsters that struck fear into the hearts of mortal men; sometimes they even caused the gods trouble. At the same time, there were many heroes of legend—sons of the gods—who fought against these beasts in order to preserve their cities, their loves, and glory. In many cases, these heroes also end up deified and given a seat or at least, offered one, in Olympus.

Heracles and the Hydra

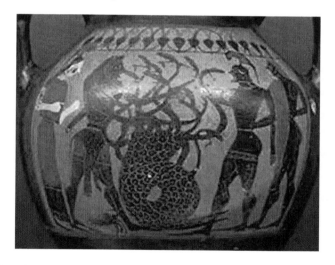

The Hydra is a gigantic water-serpent who had nine heads. It haunted the swamps of Lerna and caused dread among those who resided in the place. Heracles was sent to destroy her, a task that is part of his twelve labors.

A relatively easy task for the famed hero except the hydra had one very special attribute that he did not expect. For every head he was able to decapitate, two more sprouted in its place.

Upon learning this, he sought the help of Iolaos and applied burning pieces of wood to every severed stump, effectively cauterizing the wounds and preventing it from regenerating. In this same battle, Heracles also defeated a giant crab that came to assist the hydra.

Upon their death, the crab and the hydra were given places among the stars by Hera. We now know them as the constellations of Hydra and Cancer.

Medusa and Theseus

We've already learned about how Medusa came to be as she is, but we know nothing about the aftermath.

The Gorgons are three very powerful winged daimones. They are Medusa, Euryale, and Sthenno—among them, only Medusa is mortal.

The Gorgons were often depicted as winged women with serpents for hair, wide mouths, tusks similar to that of a wild boar, and large piercing eyes. It is said that just one glance towards them can turn a person into stone.

It is for this reason that King Polydektes of Seriphos commanded Perseus to bring back Medusa's head. A task which he accomplished with some help from the gods; they equipped him with a curved sword, a reflective shield, the helm of invisibility, and winged boots.

As the story goes, Perseus was successful in his task and he put Medusa's head in a sack as he fled, her two sisters chasing after him as he went.

The Sphinx and Oedipus

The Sphinx was a female monster that had the body of a lion, eagle's wings, the head and breast of a woman, and in some texts, she also had a serpent's tail. The gods, in fact, sent her as a plague to the town of Thebes as punishment, and she preyed on the youth by devouring all of those who are unable to solve the riddle she presents them with.

King Creon of Thebes, the city's regent, offered the throne to the person who would be able to destroy her. Oedipus took on the challenge and she gave him the riddle, one that she learned from the muses, thinking that he would end up like all the others who had tried before. However, Oedipus successfully answered her and in distress, the Sphinx threw herself off of the mountainside.

The Minotaur and Theseus

The Minotaur is a bull-headed monster that was born to Queen Pasiphae of Crete. Because of its monstrosity and viciousness, was kept in a twisting labyrinth where regular sacrifices were made to it in the form of maidens and youths.

These sacrifices were made against the will of the Athenians but were obliged to provide as tribute to King Minos.

The Minotaur was actually named Asterios when it was born and is often depicted as a human who had the face of a bull. That is, his body is completely human save for his head. The labyrinth it was kept in was designed by Daedalus in such a way that there would be no escape after one has entered it.

Theseus was sent to slay the beast and he successfully did so, leaving him with only the challenge of escaping the labyrinth left. For this, he had Ariadne's help. She provided him with thread, which allowed him to retrace his footsteps back to the exit.

The Legendary Gryphon

Though conflicts between these creatures and Greek heroes aren't oft mentioned, these majestic beasts have been portrayed and referenced countless times in various forms throughout the centuries. The Gryphon was once thought as the king of all creatures, mixing the most powerful of all mammals, the lion, and the king of all birds, the eagle. They are known to have the head and wings of an eagle and the body of a lion. At times they can be depicted as either having talons or claws.

Known as hoarders of treasure they are thought to keep mounds of gold and precious artifacts contained within their nests, hidden alongside their brood in burrows. They are also known to be a little greedy and to continue to seek these possessions out, digging them from nearby mining shafts and gold veins.

They are thought to reside along the edges and crags of the Scythian Mountains. Their neighbors, the one-eyed Arimaspians or Arimaspoi, hungrily eyed their trove of valuables and artifacts from afar. In an effort to steal the lot the Arimaspians mounted horses and continuously fought them over these treasures.

It is also often thought that these mighty birds pulled Apollo's chariot as he traveled between the earth and the sun. Throughout history they have been the symbol of both wisdom and power, which would have been fitting for Apollo, the sun god, who also epitomized wisdom through knowledge.

Chapter 6: Remnants of Greek Mythology

Though it's been ages ago since the gods of Greek Myth have held any sway upon mankind, their influence remains palpable even to this day. The Ancient Greeks who built great temples and tributes for them have managed to preserve, in great detail, several key pieces. These pieces weren't just simple texts and stories; they were also major works consisting of archaeology and art.

Many of their places of worship and cities that they presided over still stand, and can be visited and touched. Below, we enumerate a few:

THE ACROPOLIS

The Acropolis is an ancient citadel located right on an outcrop that overlooks the city of Athens. Within it, one will find what remains of several ancient structures, many of which were dedicated to the gods. Among the ruins there are:

- **The Parthenon**: This was a temple dedicated to the goddess Athena, who was also the Athenian people's patron. Despite its current state, it continues to be considered an enduring symbol of Athenian democracy, and that of the western civilizations. It has gone through a number of changes and even survived numerous attacks. These days, restoration programs are ongoing to preserve the structure and its stability, ensuring that it would be around for years to come.

- ***The Erectheion***. This is another temple on the Acropolis, which was dedicated to both Poseidon and Athena. In some texts, it is said to have been built as a tribute to King Erechtheus, but the widely accepted theory is that it was erected for the gods. It must be noted that the entire temple is on a slope, meaning its northern and western sides are a few meters lower than the southern and eastern sides—the fact that it still stands is a testament to the craftsmanship of its builders.

THE TEMPLE OF ZEUS, OLYMPIA

You may not be able to visit the original building, but in its plot, there still stands a second temple, which was modeled after the first. Some of it may lie in ruins, whilst other parts remain buried, but this once grandiose temple was once home to the statue of Zeus—one of the seven wonders of the Ancient World.

It is said that the Chryselephantine (a statue of gold and ivory) was about 13 m in height and was crafted by Phidias, taking him 12 years to complete it.

DELPHI

We know of Delphi as the place wherein a great oracle, guided by Apollo, resided. Many think of it as piece of land where heaven and earth once met, were divine prophecies were made. Within it, much like in the Acropolis, are many places of worship for the gods and goddesses—which is also the reason why some people consider it to be a sacred land.

Today, there's still plenty to be seen from the Ancient city. The Temple of Apollo survives, along with a different theater and athletic structures. A gymnasium and stadium all call back to the Pythian Games, comparable to today's Olympics, where competitors from all the farthest corners of Greece met to compete for titles and glory.

Chapter 7: Greek Mythology in Art and Modernity

The influence of Greek Mythology isn't just confined within the boundaries of Greece. You may be aware of the fact that each of these Grecian gods and goddesses all have Roman counterparts—different in name, but mostly similar in purpose and function.

When it came to art, Greek Mythology has inspired many great artists—this is most evident when it comes to classical paintings. Many artists turned to these myths and depicted the epic tales upon canvas, bringing to life stories, which were once only shared by word of mouth.

"Psyche Revived by Cupid's Kiss"

In this marble sculpture by Antonio Canova, we see Psyche reaching up to her divine lover after having been awakened. It is said that Psyche had opened a jar containing "Sleep of the Innermost Darkness" which then penetrated her entire body, leaving her unconscious on the spot.

Cupid revives his beloved with a kiss and a prick of his arrow. The brief moment of her awakening is forever captured in this depiction.

The sculpture is currently housed in the Louvre.

Winged Victory of Samothrace (Nike)

This marble sculpture can trace its origins to 2nd century BC and has been referred to as one of "the greatest masterpiece of

Hellenistic sculpture". It is known to be one of the very few original Hellenistic statues as the others are Roman copies.

The statue stands at 244 centimeters and was not only created in tribute to the goddess, Nike, it was also meant to honor a sea battle. The flowing drapery of the dress and the form of the goddess, seemingly descending from the heavens, is truly a sight to behold.

At its base, the inscription "Rhodios" can be found which points to the statue as being commissioned for a naval victory by Rhodes.

Greek Mythology as We Know It

We also find traces of Greek Mythology in science, where names of certain things have been taken from that of the gods. A great example of this would be the names of the various moons orbiting planets throughout our solar system, many of which have been taken from the various characters of myth. Some of these names are **Phobos, Deimos, Rhea,** and **Pandora.**

However, it is in literature and film, where the ancient gods and goddesses of Greek Mythology have managed to truly achieve immortality. They still remain a popular subject or inspiration for many modern stories, often given personalities and characterizations that match the time the book was written. We may remember them from when we first experienced the animated or live action variants of Hercules in theatres to reading amazing books like Rick Riordan's Percy Jackson, J.K. Rowling's Harry Potter, and J.R.R. Tolkien's The Lord of the Rings. We even see cameos of them in such hit comedy shows like Family Guy. In truth Hercules was actually a Roman hero and god. Heracles was his Greek equivalent and his father was actually Jupiter, who was the Roman equivalent of Zeus.

In other instances we have been exposed to Greek Mythology almost on a daily basis without ever having really realized it. The famous shoe and sports wear brand, Nike, was actually named after the goddess of Victory, who aided Zeus in his war against the Titans during Titanomachy.

It is for these reasons why we're all so familiar with much of the Greek pantheon. Their influence is palpable in quite a few mediums, and though we don't necessarily provide them with worship like the Ancient Greeks did before, it goes without saying that the gods and goddesses, and all other divine beings of myth are truly alive even in this age.

And that, without a doubt, is the real power of Greek Mythology.

Conclusion

Thank you so much for reading until the end of this book!

I really hope this book was able to help you get familiar with some of the many gods, goddesses, and other prominent figures littered throughout Greek Mythology as well as the level of significance they were afforded during ancient times. Greek art and mythology will continue to amaze, captivate, and astonish audiences around the world and hopefully, continue to weave traces of inspiration in modern works well into the future.

For those of you who absolutely love this and want to dive deeper into the wide world of Greek Mythology, I've included a bibliography. Also, if you have any questions or comments for me regarding this book please feel free to contact me at helpfulbookideas@gmail.com.

Finally, if you enjoyed this book, then I'd like to ask you for a favor, would you be kind enough to leave a review for this book on Amazon? It'd be greatly appreciated!

Thank you and stay tuned for more of my books on history and mythology covering various cultures!

Check Out My Other Books

Below you'll find some of my other popular books that are on Amazon and Kindle as well. Alternatively, you can visit my author page on Amazon to see other work done by me.

Norse Mythology – The Heroes, Gods, Sagas, Beliefs, and Rituals of Nordic Mythology

Printed in Great Britain
by Amazon